Parts & Labor

PARTS & LABOR

POEMS

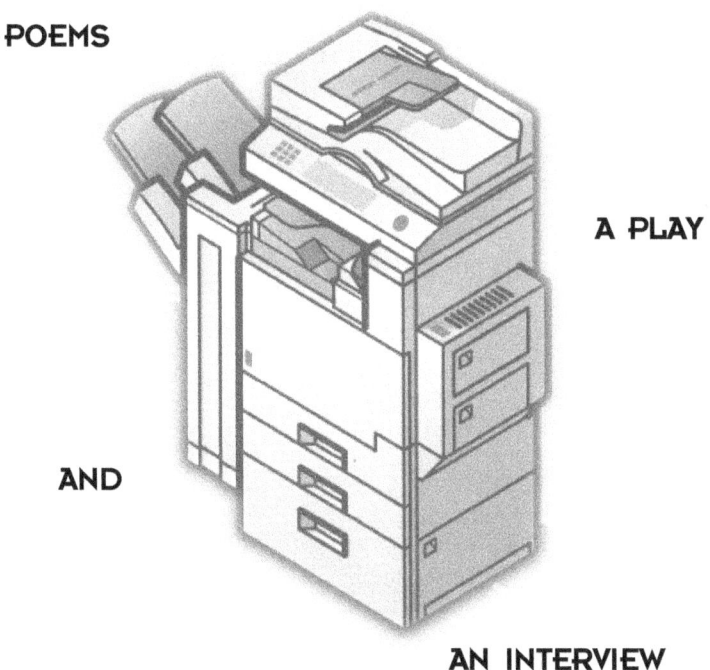

A PLAY

AND

AN INTERVIEW

GREGORY HISCHAK

Pond Road Press   Washington D.C.   North Truro, Massachusetts

Copyright © 2012 by Gregory Hischak
All rights reserved

Published by Pond Road Press

Printed in the United States of America by Lightning Source Inc.

Distributed through the Ingram Book Company, and in turn available online from Amazon and Barnes & Noble, as well as directly from Pond Road Press.

The word mark, logo, and configuration of the Etch A Sketch product are registered trademarks of the Ohio Art Company.

ISBN: 978-0-9719741-4-2

Library of Congress Control Number: 2012931896

Cover art by illustrator Peter Willems

Book design and layout by Patric Pepper

Author photos by Brittainy Botelho (back cover) and Gregory Hischak (inside bio)

Display font: Insignia LT
Text font: Garamond

Pond Road Press
221 Channing Street NE
Washington, DC 20002

www.pondroadpress.com
pondroadpress@hotmail.com

To Tom,
who has kept the bookshelf
filled from the beginning

CONTENTS

Preflight

1. The Temperature on Mercury

Caroline 3
Terms 4
Firm 5
Assembly 6
Closure 7
Hidden Driveway Lake 8
The Assistant 9
Imperfect Stone 10
The Alluvial Hour 11
The Center Ring 12
Cuban Missile Crisis 13
The Culling 14
Daylight Savings Time
    Depository 15
The Temperature on Mercury 16
Suspect Yield 17
Temporary Shelter 18
Poetry in the Cars 19

2. Poor Shem

    A Play for Three Characters
        and Photocopier

3. The Night of this Place

The Night of this Place 37
Erratica 38
Appalachian Spring 39

Powering Down   40
Atlantic Flyway   41
Obsolescence   42
The Egyptian Wing   43
The Late Shift   44
Swimming Lesson   45
Waning Gibbous
    Over Hidden Driveway Lake   46
The Custodians   47
The Baptismal Font   48
Senior Night Game   49
Parts & Labor   50

High Energy and Many Hats
An Interview with Gregory Hischak   53

Acknowledgements
About the Author
Colophon

Parts & Labor

PREFLIGHT

In the event of a loss of cabin pressure
a poem will descend from the ceiling

To alleviate any panic or shortness of breath
press the poem to your ear—hold it to your mouth

Grasp the poem firmly before applying it
to the inner child traveling with you

Be forewarned that it is against federal regulations
to tamper with the allegory of the poem

Remember that some shifting of contents overhead
is not unheard of

Consider that the integrity of the poem may fail you
that its final destination may become questionable

Consider that the nearest emergency exit
is already far behind you

In the unlikely event of a water landing
the poem may be used as a flotation device

1. The Temperature on Mercury

CAROLINE

Don't believe everything you've read about me
Caroline said as she taped me to her chair
I hadn't read anything about her actually
but I was beginning to think that I should have
Maybe paid more attention to those posts
    than I did

Still—I liked her style and her laugh and her delight
in all that glowed dark and disorderly
and I appreciated the calm stately perversion
that was someday going to make someone
    very happy
I would have told her all this had she not warned me
that the merest utterance from my lips would be my last

I bumped into Caroline a few weeks later
outside the coffee shop—or at the Red Box
or rummaging through the ossuary
    the details blur—she didn't recognize me
but I knew it was Caroline by her uniform
—by the cold warping of time and matter shimmering
in her wake—by her laugh

TERMS

I have allowed my extended warranty to lapse
—my personal factory powertrain warranty
from its forty-eight thousand mile fifty-one year
protection plan I am cut adrift

The alignment of moral compasses
the proper disposal of previously held opinions
convictions and lubricants—as covered
under the terms of my warranty—void
I am now at liberty to indulge in acts of war
to perform irregular maintenance
to engage in commercial use or not
      —it is my choice

The normal wear and tear I will be subject to
I will take like a man—without a good neighbor
and when I fall to pieces I will lie like a man
lies in pieces across that gravel shoulder
      —stripped of my parts and labors
disengaged from drive—this odometer
released of its miles to go—this heart
freed of its promises to keep

FIRM

We discovered Shem outside his cubicle that morning
chest cavity split—spinal column snapped
like a number 2 pencil—a splash of viscera across
the mauve carpet—there had been talk around the firm
outside of accounts payable there were sightings—
spreadsheets masticated by powerful jaws—a gash
across countertops where previously no gash had been

    —Monica thought she saw cubs

We'd been told to whistle when walking the hallways
alone now—to make ourselves heard and every hour
I prayed for my day to end peacefully
    without carnage—prayed
that I'd be allowed to expire quietly
in some interstate pile-up—not gracelessly torn
    limb from limb

Noticing my agitation—a superior called me in
    Of all the things that you could give in life
Rob said—*nothing is more precious than your labor*
—*the job you will dedicate your best*
your most productive years to
    Rob then asked me to close his office door

He worked swiftly—a swipe and a rending
a heartfelt vivisection—a lithe economy of gestures
reducing a once durable link in this food chain
into something soft and pink—expendable

ASSEMBLY

It was the umpteenth beginning
the someteenth creation
following closely again upon the heels
of the previous—someone said
it was yet another whole new ballgame

Mountains and pandas and universal joints
would be created on Monday
while asphalt and cork and meringue
would be formed on Tuesday
Wednesday would be a day of rest
Thursday saw heavy water
extension cords and mayonnaise
come into being—it was all assembling
     very nicely this time
On Friday power saws and full moons
salad spinners and people would all be
cranked out for the long weekend ahead

All over again everything would need naming
    We shall call this Saturday Night
the newly formed people would say
awaiting the dusk
and their falls from grace to begin

CLOSURE

They're working on the closure again
punching a 17-lane haiku past the Appleby's
bolting metaphors to bridge spans
retrofitting the allegory
to handle a big one

Poets are out working for the county
deviating the westbound flow
    Couplet in Road Ahead
hammering at the iambic on Saturday
for time and a half

It's traffic cones and semicolons and
stopping by woods—stopping by woods—
    stopping by woods
all the way to Wareham
it's one big ugly open mic

In a shower of locution
poets are welding the grid
paving the gaps and flagging you
to roll down the window—listen
to the stories turning these wheels

HIDDEN DRIVEWAY LAKE

Slack foster care and improper drainage—
that's what caseworkers will mumble
when asked about Hidden Driveway Lake
a feral body of purulence and murk roving
from bottomland to Walmart lot and back

Prodded along by an army corps of engineers
chased out of town with a shovel and ditch
slipping through Terre Haute like a slow leak
losing clarity in the cataracts of Sioux Falls
a pool of lost potential—Hidden Driveway Lake

Running its downward slope from first drink
to last drop spilt in some Bakersfield culvert
I let a dime fall to its tan foam and shudder
What if I had sprung from such headwaters?
What if my world were to tilt just so?

THE ASSISTANT

She submits a little too easily to being sawn in half—
    I often think in the shower
my trailer drain clogged with her sequins
good towels hexed with mascara and glitter
fishnets cast across a closet doorknob

She's a coo of doves from a trick deck of cards
reappearing from behind her shimmering blue veil
a beguiler of swords—a backstage straightener
of collars as she discerns the house
as she lies beside me

She complies easily to the geometry of cabinets—
    I muse as she enters the kitchen
to conjure Cremora from a lazy susan of Isis
to vanish in a Marlboro plume of abracadabra
—the woman who was there and then gone
and then there again
    Reflection—
she intones—*is all done with mirrors*

Stirring a potion of black arts and volumizer
she laughs incantations from the sink
cradles a travel mug of enigma—moves closer
    Illusion—
she whispers—*is a thin dark seam drawn
up the back of a woman's white leg*

IMPERFECT STONE

Consider for a moment
that debris
swept to Michelangelo's curbside
stepped across
the less than perfect stone
chipped from his *David*
truncated shavings
misfit flakes in the company
of like talus and similar rubble
the reduced and culled
of yet another masterwork

What if you had been that last shard
    of almost?
a fixture till the end
the last sliver of Carrara
chiseled from the tip of that nose
that perfect nose
freed from its stone
made divine
by your absence

THE ALLUVIAL HOUR

Embedded in facades along Fourth Avenue
    trilobites and nautiloids
frozen in the facing stone
    brine shrimp and starfish
I'm a pawn in geology's game here
    a relic
a striation of wrinkled brows scratched
    in some shopfront glass
walking a canyon grid gouged by
    the stiff current of five o'clock shadows
There's a click to my step
    a weight to my stride—
a stowaway pebble hugs the tread
    of my Rockports
I'm moving a coastal range uptown
    one stone at a time

THE CENTER RING

They smile an awful lot
    that family
for living on such a tightrope
    that acrobat family
the joined weight of acrobat mothers
    and acrobat daughters
catapulting acrobat sons into chairs held aloft
    by acrobat fathers—on unicycles
unicycles on cables—cables without nets
I want to spend the holidays with this family
    this acrobat family
the taut hurtles of their pins and needles
and bones and secrets

    They have no secrets

Their grasp of physics unbreakable
the laundry and cat food of this acrobat family
juggled with aplomb—unflappable
    And here—in this ring
    my family
firmly mired in our gravities—unsmiling
our assemblies conducted without ovation
    or poise
    or tight red shirts
reasonably sure that in our tumbles through air
hands will be there waiting
    never quite sure whose

CUBAN MISSILE CRISIS

It was Saturday that my older brothers and Eric Roller
built a dam in the back gully—shopping cart frames
stink mud and dirt clods and jabbed through with a
rusty spine of swing set pole—the gully would not be
safe for me—my brothers explained—suggesting
my ducking and my covering be done at home

All week the crick backed up—flooding the gully
all the way to the Mt. Read Boulevard culvert
the rising waters dark with October tannins
the previously dry and firm now squishy
lapping at the stairs—inundations of black
and white bulletins—a murky silence that eddied
     around the Magnavox

Two gray Sundays passed before word of the dam
finally reached the President and Dad yelled outside
to my brothers and Eric Roller to get down to the gully
and knock the damn dam down—they did—I think
all of us aware that some brink had been faced
and then stepped back from

THE CULLING

*You can tell they're senior by the thickness
of their coats*—my father whispered as three males
and three females emerged from the stand of aspens

They shuffled protectively surrounding two interns
petite and fawn-like—probably just hired that spring
as one of the males turned—warm steam billowing
from his toothy grin—and waved a small card at us

Travis Melich—Senior Account Coordinator

he shouted and he indeed seemed the most senior
of this herd of senior account coordinators

Driving home that evening—Travis' card tucked
in the driver's side visor—I asked my father
      how it felt to pull that trigger
as a systems analyst scurried into the path of our
      hurtling radials
Always exercise your authority—my father explained
accelerating toward contact—*or risk your authority
      going soft*

DAYLIGHT SAVINGS TIME DEPOSITORY

Here is the facility where they are kept
those lustrous ingots of hours
bars of semiprecious minutes
sealed in vaults locked in drawers
the sun-filled hours garnished from spring
collated and boxed and stored in this secured warehouse
    on the outskirts of Greenwich

The Daylight Savings Time Depository
a nondescript building—timeless you might say

In a small lobby—its walls a clutter of
    clocks and ticks—
the security guard sits behind his desk
He wears a crisp blue uniform
gives a crisp blue *No* when asked
for that hour taken to be returned
says *No* when it is explained how
within that extracted hour
what I had allowed to drop
might be retrieved—given the time
the security guard shakes his head
says *No*
says *Maybe in the fall*
but probably
No

THE TEMPERATURE ON MERCURY

During the course of a day here on Mercury
temperature fluctuates between terrible extremes
from nights of -320°F—where even out of the wind
every night is the coldest night of the year to days
of 930°F—where even in the shade it's hot
and here on a planet totally devoid of even trace amounts
of Fresca—930° can sometimes seem like 940°

But keep in mind those twenty minutes in the morning
and again those twenty minutes of late afternoon when
between these terrible extremes of temperature
it's really *not* so bad out—consider that twice a day
here on Mercury there's opportunity for a short stroll
or maybe a coffee—a hot beverage enjoyed in the glow
     of a rising sun
perhaps a cold beverage quietly sipped
between the lengthening shadows—just you and I

We've always had these handful of minutes
     here on Mercury
tucked between pan-seared day and freezer-burned night
these windows of opportunity offered us—you and I
     here on Mercury
always entrusting within these twenty or so minutes
twice a day—everything

SUSPECT YIELD

What river lies here
contained in this apple
diverted into this strawberry
siphoned from the Colorado
the Sacramento
bled from the Rio Bravo
the Concho
the Pecos and the Green?

Was it a transfusion of Rio Grande
or Yakima that stayed the life
of this avocado
this still life of suspect yield
landscape with field hand
spigot of thick brown water
running the shallows and wire
of border country?

What rouge horde have I placed
on this checkout scanner
this culpable fruit
sloshing captive against
the cistern mesh
of my reusable bag?

TEMPORARY SHELTER

The frozen food aisle recedes
eight feet a year now—
so long snapper and cod
     so long Sea Nuggets
Tater Tots and Klondike Bars
A viscous flow of molten carrot
snakes the length of driveway
hisses into encroaching sea
     —adieu Vegetable Medley

Under a borealis of tepid rain
my daughter releases our bag of party ice
into the surf
Her future now a future of farmed ice
she scans the thickening haze
squints the bobbing shine of angles northward
     —so long cubes

We stop at the gymnasium on our way home
to say goodnight to Sara Lee
pause beside the damp cot of Mrs. Paul
wipe her fevered brow
whisper her thawing bones to crowded rest
murmur godspeed

POETRY IN THE CARS

Hunched and squirming in their cars
everybody is muttering poetry to themselves

That's what I tell my daughter after sitting in traffic
for 45 minutes outside Braintree or Quincy or somewhere

But Dad—she says from her plaid Mary Oliver booster seat
—*all their poetry seems really angry*—and so I explain

that sometimes poetry is angry poetry—sometimes
poetry scowls and turns its back on rainbows

sometimes poetry just wants to slap the horn—sometimes
poetry crawls like a dirge

The guy with the Vermont plates trying to cut me off
is spewing Bukowski

Some Xfinity van is Ginsberging the best minds
of his generation right on my ass

A middle finger extended from my driver side window
has Emily Dickinson all over it

The lady driving the Forester in front of us—
thinning gray hair barely visible above her seat

I can tell from the breath on her windshield
she's mumbling a haiku—

> still against my gaze
> the empty lane before me
> fills with swerving cars

Oh my God—are you going to Go or What—lady?
and my daughter asks—*What poem are you reciting, Dad?*

It's Whitman
"Are You Going To Go Or What, Lady" by Walt Whitman

What's it about? she asks when I think I'm off the hook
And so I tell her—I tell her it's about movement

it's about snaking the s-curves the way we snaked
out of Eden on that first morning commute

it's about the momentum that propels us forward
powered by gasoline and the fear of being left behind

it's about manifest destiny outside Braintree or Quincy
or somewhere at about 15 mph

it's about how when that strand of brake lights cuts
the haze—when the dawn strikes cold hard chrome

when the shimmer and bend of a guardrail is the only
moral compass left to you, child—*that's* poetry

that's what it's about

2. Poor Shem

POOR SHEM

A PLAY FOR THREE CHARACTERS AND PHOTOCOPIER

Characters:
    Kendel a dominant male, 35 to 55
    Kaitlin a woman of easily diluted compassion, 25 to 55
    Kyle   a less dominant male—probably younger than
           Kendel, 30 to 40

The setting is an office copying room. Present day.
Text Note: tabbed type in the script indicates an overlap of dialogue.

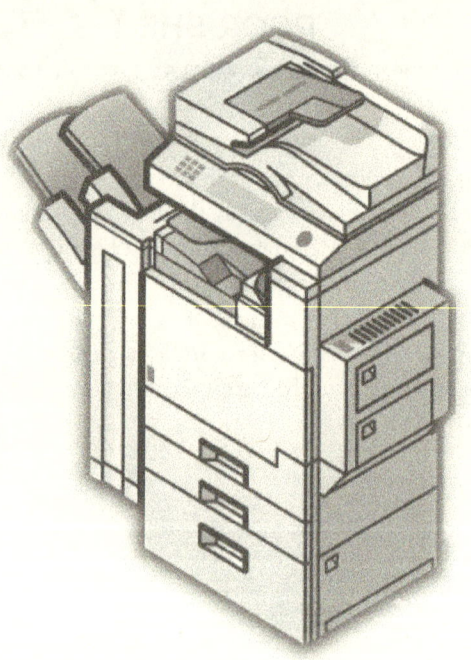

(*Machinery sounds—these are performed by the characters.*)
KENDEL   Shicka shicka shicka shicka . . . *(Continue as*
         KAITLIN joins in.)
KAITLIN Fwoosha ha fwoosha ha fwoosha ha fwoosha ha . . .
         (Continue as KYLE joins in.)
KYLE   Kahlakala kahlakala kahlakala kahlakala kahlakala
         kahlakala kahlakala klahk.
         (All stop.)
KAITLIN Of all the things you give in your life, none is more
         precious than your labor.
KYLE   The job you are paid to do.
KENDEL   The job you dedicate your best,
                        most productive years to.
         (Beat.)
KENDEL   Shicka shicka shicka shicka . . . *(Continue as*
         KAITLIN joins in.)
KAITLIN Fwoosha ha fwoosha ha fwoosha ha fwoosha ha . . .
         (Continue as KYLE joins in.)
KYLE   Kahlakala kahlakala kahlakala kahlakala kahlakala
         kahlakala kahlakala klahk.
         (Abrupt pained all stop.)

KAITLIN Jesus.
KYLE   Don't that beat—
KENDEL   Shit.
KAITLIN For the love of—
KYLE   I'll be damned.
KAITLIN Jammed.
KENDEL   Jammed?
KYLE   What happened?
KAITLIN Jammed.
KYLE   Who jammed it?
KAITLIN *Nobody* jammed it.
KYLE   It just jammed?
KENDEL   Yes, jammed.
KAITLIN It *just* jammed.
KENDEL   Christ.
KAITLIN   Christ.

KYLE   There's an eight and a half by eleven stuck in the by-pass tray.

              (Thoughtful beat.)
KENDEL   An 8 1/2 x 11 stuck in the by-pass tray?
KYLE   It says so right here . . .
KAITLIN   Try hitting Print again.
KYLE   Don't hit Print.
KENDEL   There's an 8 1/2 x 11 stuck in the by-pass tray.
KAITLIN   Push the Green Button.
KYLE   Don't push the Green Button, you'll kill us all.
KENDEL   Let's not panic, people.
KAITLIN   Christ.
KYLE   What do we do?
KENDEL   Open the front panel.
KYLE   What?
KAITLIN   Right. Open the front of the copier.
KYLE   *I'm* not opening the front of the copier.
              (The following spoken in unison.)
KAITLIN   Do I look like I'm dressed to open copiers?
KENDEL   It's not my job to open the front of
                        the copier to fix every goddamned
                        paper jam . . . Jesus.
              (KYLE has opened the copier.)
KAITLIN   For the love of . . .
KENDEL   I'll be damned.
              (Thoughtful beat.)
KYLE   That's a jam.
KENDEL   That is *one hell* of a jam.
KAITLIN   What is that?
KENDEL   *One hell* of a jam.
KAITLIN   No, that.
KYLE   What?
KAITLIN   That.
KYLE   You mean right *there?*
KAITLIN   No, *that* right there.
KENDEL   There?
KYLE   There?

KAITLIN   Yeah, right *there*.
KENDEL   What is that?
KYLE   *That?*
KAITLIN   Yes, *that*.
KYLE   That's my abutments and drainage proposal.
KAITLIN   No. What's that wrapped around it?
KYLE   *There?*
KAITLIN   THERE.
KENDEL   That's a tie.

(Thoughtful beat.)
KAITLIN   It's a necktie
KENDEL   Yup, that's a necktie all right.
KYLE   It's a yellow necktie with . . . a . . .
KAITLIN   So, what's *that* then?
KYLE   You mean right—
KAITLIN   There.
KENDEL   Inside the necktie?
KAITLIN   Right there inside the necktie.
KYLE   That would be . . .
   (Beat.)
KENDEL   It's a neck.

   (Beat for examination.)
KYLE   Yup, that's a neck all right.
KAITLIN   It's a neck.
KYLE   That's a neck in that tie.
KENDEL   Yup.
   (Beat.)
KAITLIN   So, it stands to reason that this . . . this neck is attached . . . to *something?*
KENDEL   Absolutely.
KYLE   No way around it.
KENDEL   Necks don't just happen.
KAITLIN   So, what's that attached—
KENDEL   To the neck—?
KYLE   *That* neck?
KAITLIN   Of course *that* neck.

KENDEL Do you see another neck in there—?
KYLE   It's Shem.

(Thoughtful beat.)
KENDEL What?
KYLE   Shem.
KAITLIN   That's Shem all right.
KENDEL *(addressing SHEM)* Shem?
KYLE   *(addressing SHEM)* Shem?

(Thoughtful beat.)
KAITLIN Jesus
KYLE   Don't that beat—
KENDEL   Shit.
KYLE   It's Shem, all right.
KAITLIN *(Addressing SHEM)* Shem?
KENDEL Shem's in the copier.
KYLE   That's Shem's tie.
KENDEL How do you know that's Shem's tie?
KYLE   I bought Shem that tie.
KENDEL You *bought* him that tie?
KAITLIN That's Shem's tie all right. Poor Shem.
KENDEL What do you mean you bought him that tie?
KYLE   It was a present.
KENDEL A present?
KAITLIN How thoughtful. Birthday?
KYLE   Secret Santa.
KENDEL Poor Shem.
KAITLIN   Poor Shem.
KYLE   Poor Shem. *(addressing SHEM)* Shem?

(Thoughtful beat.)
KAITLIN He's dead isn't he?
KENDEL Very much so.
KAITLIN   Shem is dead.
KYLE   Crushed to death in the 8 1/2 x 11 by-pass tray.
KAITLIN Asphyxiated.
KENDEL Decapitated.

KYLE   Mangled.
KAITLIN   Electrocuted.
KENDEL   Collated.
KAITLIN   Poor Shem.
KYLE   Poor Shem.

            (Respectful beat.)
KAITLIN   How old was he?
KYLE   Thirty-four.
KAITLIN   *Only* thirty-four.
KYLE   His whole life ahead of him.
KENDEL   Apparently not.
KYLE   We should get him out.
KAITLIN   It's the right thing to do.
KYLE   He'd have done it for any one of us.
KENDEL   How do you know that?
KYLE   He was that kind of man.
KENDEL   *What* kind of man?
KAITLIN   Did you say birthday?
KYLE   Secret Santa.
KAITLIN   It's very nice.
KENDEL   Yes, nice tie, Kyle.
KYLE   Thank you.
KAITLIN   Stylish.
            (Beat.)
KENDEL   So, why is it—?
KYLE   What?
KENDEL   Why is it—we don't have interns for cleaning up messes like this?
KYLE   An intern is an excellent idea.
KAITLIN   On-the-job training.
KYLE   It develops those people skills.
KENDEL   Priceless skills for later . . . in life.
KAITLIN   in life—poor Shem.
KYLE   Struck down in his prime.
KAITLIN   You just *never* know.
KENDEL   Know what?
KAITLIN   Life.

KENDEL	Oh, that.
KAITLIN	Blink.
KYLE	That's right, blink.
KENDEL	Blink?
KAITLIN	It's that quick.
KENDEL	Look at the time.
KYLE	How did it get to be lunchtime?
KAITLIN	Poor Shem.
KENDEL	It's . . . *really* not my job . . . I mean—scraping Shem from the copier.
KAITLIN	Do I look like I'm dressed for—
KYLE	Drainage and abutments, that's my job. Poor Shem.
KAITLIN	Poor ol' Shem. We should call his wife.
KENDEL	We should call the copier repairman.
KYLE	Morrie?
KENDEL	Morrie.
KAITLIN	Yes, we should call Morrie.
KENDEL	Morrie will know what to do.
KYLE	Morrie knows his copiers.
KAITLIN	Somebody should call Shem's wife. She'd want to know.
KENDEL	It's not my job to tell people that their husbands were sucked into photocopiers.
KAITLIN	She'd want to know.
KENDEL	It's the right thing to do.
KYLE	Poor Shem.
KENDEL	Poor Shem.
KAITLIN	Poor ol' Shem.

(Longer thoughtful beat.)

KENDEL	Did Shem *have* a wife?
KYLE	No. I mean, I don't *think* so . . .
KENDEL	No wife?
KAITLIN	With a tie like that—and no wife?
KENDEL	Hard to believe, isn't it?
KYLE	It is.

	(Beat.)
KENDEL	So then . . .
KYLE	Well . . .
KAITLIN	There you are.
KENDEL	Yup.
KYLE	Poor Shem.
KAITLIN	Poor Shem.
KENDEL	Poor Shem—you know . . . maybe . . .
KYLE	Maybe—?
KAITLIN	Maybe . . .what?
KENDEL	Maybe the 8 1/2 x 14 tray is working?
KAITLIN	*(Mild outrage.)* What?
KENDEL	I mean Shem is stuck in the 8 1/2 x 11 by-pass tray—
KYLE	Tragically mutilated in an 8 1/2 x 11 by-pass tray.
KAITLIN	*(Mild outrage.)* A co-worker is dead here.
KENDEL	Yes, poor Shem.
KYLE	Poor ol' Shem—you've got a point, though.
KENDEL	That's right
KYLE	The 8 1/2 x 14 tray *might* be working.
KAITLIN	A *co-worker* is dead here.
KYLE	We should call Morrie.
KENDEL	Hit the 8 1/2 x 14, people.
KAITLIN	Maybe we should call a priest.
KYLE	No, we should call Morrie.
KAITLIN	Morrie is not ordained.
KYLE	Morrie knows his copiers.
KENDEL	No, hit the Reset first.
KAITLIN	We should call a priest.
KENDEL	Hit the Reset first.
KYLE	Maybe we should call Morrie *and* a priest.
KAITLIN	A co-worker is dead.
KYLE	I know. Do I hit Reset or call a priest? *(Beat.)* Do I hit Reset or call a priest?
	(Thoughtful beat for moral dilemma.)
KYLE	Reset, or a priest?
	(Thoughtful beat for moral dilemma.)

KYLE   Reset, or a priest, Kaitlin?

            (Thoughtful beat for moral dilemma.)
KYLE   Kendel, Reset, or a priest?

            (Longer thoughtful beat for moral dilemma.)
KENDEL   Reset.
KYLE   Reset?
KAITLIN   Reset.
KENDEL   Close the front panel, Kyle.
KYLE   You close the panel, Kaitlin.
KAITLIN   Do I look like I'm dressed for closing the front panel?
KENDEL   Close the front panel, Kyle.
KYLE   I'm closing the front panel then.
KAITLIN   Okay. Hit 8 1/2 x 14, Kyle.
KENDEL   No, hit the Reset first.
KAITLIN   Hit Print.
KENDEL   *Don't hit Print.* You waste your time hitting Print until the copier is warmed up.
KAITLIN   A co-worker is dead.
KYLE   He had his whole life ahead of him.
KENDEL   Tragically mutilated in an 8 1/2 x 11 bypass tray.
KAITLIN   Of all the things you could give in your life, none is more precious than your labor.
KYLE   Your labor—
KENDEL   Hit Reset again.
KYLE   —is the most precious. The job you are paid to do; the job you dedicate the best, most productive years of your life to. Nothing is more precious than that.
KENDEL   *I've* always believed that.
KAITLIN   I've *always* believed that.
KYLE   *Nothing* is more precious than that.

            (Thoughtful beat.)
KENDEL   So, we'll wait for the Green Button to light up.

KAITLIN   And when it lights up—
KYLE   —we'll hit Print.
KENDEL   Wait for the Green.
KYLE   I'm waiting for the Green.
KENDEL   It's warming up . . . it's warming . . .
KAITLIN   Let it warm up.
KYLE   I'm *letting* it warm up, already.
KENDEL   Wait for the Green.
KAITLIN   And when it turns Green.
KYLE   We'll hit Print.
KENDEL   Almost lunchtime.
KYLE   I'm starved.
KAITLIN   Wait for it.
KYLE   I'm waiting.
KENDEL   Wait for it.
KYLE   I'm waiting.
KENDEL   Wait for the Green.

KAITLIN   Of all the things you could give . . .
KYLE   Nothing is more precious . . .
KENDEL   I've always believed that.
KYLE   I've always believed that.
            (Beat.)
KENDEL   Shicka shicka shicka shicka . . . *(Continue as
            KAITLIN joins in.)*
KAITLIN   Fwoosha ha fwoosha ha fwoosha ha fwoosha ha . . .
            (Continue as KYLE joins in.)
KYLE   Kahlakala kahlakala kahlakala kahlakala kahlakala
            kahlakala kahlakala klahk.
            (All stop.)

KENDEL   Poor Shem.
KYLE   Poor Shem.
KAITLIN   Poor ol' Shem.

            (To black.)

            (End of play.)

3. The Night of this Place

THE NIGHT OF THIS PLACE

We know the night of this place
glowfish below and dipper above
scythe of moon through trees
I know the night of your places
and you mine
this terrain that unfolds and reveals
in shadow and dale
rakes the hillside
of its screech and rustle
its hollowed-out spaces
where we stand out of the tempest
and within the tempest
where we find our shelter

ERRATICA

Have pity on future geologists
    poor bastards
vexed by the terrain we've left them
our cairns of irreconcilable differences
    heaped from sea to shallow sea
puzzled by our random dispersal of granites
    and beach glass
by the igneous stories of our mantels
    the sedimentary banter of our tables
the tales metamorphic
    scratched across dashboards
swept from shelves or released
    to the gravel of drives
when beguiled by tectonics onward
    these keepsakes left at a field's edge—
I so pity future geologists
    stymied by our unsettled movements
this plate of pitch and heave
    gouging its trail of wall stone
its slipstream of erratica
    its wake of bellow and scorch

APPALACHIAN SPRING

First—there is ocean dried to sand and lifted to sky
folded and flooded and lifted again—Appalachia
weathered and beaten and scarred by interstate
astride which—just outside Harrisburg—northbound
sprayed across a roadcut of black Mesozoic shale—

I ♥ Brenda

For that moment I saw clearly the adolescence
shimmering in the strata like alabaster
in the striations of love-warped feldspar
in the sonic outcrops of classic rock I felt the denim
stone-washed and writhing through the terra firma

This world remains a young and heckling world
its seas shallow and its mountains naive—its zinc-white
heart sprayed across the Permian for all to ponder
lifting that snow-caked sheet to gaze upon the pale
beauty of the landform slumbering beneath

I ♥ Brenda

POWERING DOWN

It was snowing on Mars this morning
light flurries—little accumulation
a gauze-white veil across hard red clay
It's hard to imagine a snowfall that quiet
bereft of spinning tires
with neither man nor angel impressed
across that meager powder
A grimace of stones circle the yard
a ghost of dry gravel
fading across the driveway
where you had just left

When snow falls to this earth
it is a strange earth that it settles on
this abyss where the land drops away
where one pauses
contemplates the pearl sky
draws figure eights across tundra
sits in the thin shadows of antennas
an array of cold shoulders
pointed upward
voiceless
toward home

ATLANTIC FLYWAY

To her oldest she teaches patience and thrift
how to cup her palms in a McDonald's sink
to stand motionless in the shallows
    of an Ocean State Job Lot
loiter the Stop & Shop bread aisle
    with a baggy coat
It's what they call natural selection

She is a follower of an inner compass
    southward
gray dawn wall of sea to left
twilight of refineries to right
the flying V of a cracked windshield
aligned toward a cousin in Eustis
an old friend near Lakeland
a sanctuary of reeds
    at this flyway's terminus
a dish of butter on a table at a window
    a mat of welcomes

OBSOLESCENCE

Like his father before him—my father was an indentor
hammering the white hot lead into delicate clarity
carving footholds into text where none had been
    It's about the readability
he said from his big kitchen chair
    It's about the fascism of misinterpretation
    that is battled every day and never stops
he soaked his fingers in a bowl—fingers bloodied
and scarred by factory serifs—fingers that fought
the good fight for lucidity

He sat silently in his chair as I announced to the family
my new position at the bindery works
He was silent as I explained how indentation
could be achieved now with a tab

It was never my intention to remove the luster
from a man's lifework
but I was not smitten with indenting—not like I was
by the forms and signatures of assembly
by the hum of collation across well swept floors
    It isn't about collation
my father yelled from the bottom of the stairs
    It has always been about the readability
When I left that next morning for the bindery works
my father said nothing
and I did not say goodbye

THE EGYPTIAN WING

Unheeded—I'm prone to repeat myself
    my motives capricious
my pages as untranslatable as the bottom half
    of Rosetta's stump left buried under Nile sand
my crosswords engraved upon the pilasters of Karnak—
    Two vast and trunkless legs of stone
    are all that remain
    of this returning Jeopardy champ

I'm the stickman leaper of Coptic flip books
defacer of psalms and scratcher of palimpsests
    The tip of an iceberg is carved by the victors

Unheeded—I'm prone to repeat myself
    —I might have mentioned that—
my actions callous—my breath fogging the glass
    of some encased and desiccated Ramses
    So it is written—so it is done—sucker

Mine is the story of he who blinks last
my timeline—an epoch of steel and pyres
my chapters—a holocaust of deeds
the blueprint I work from—a schematic
    of rose and thorn

THE LATE SHIFT

Riding home late after work I saw Swiper
sitting alone at the back of the Number 5 bus
    to Crown Hill
orange fox in a bright blue mask
    I was reasonably sure it was him
Swiper sat staring at his reflection
    against the dark glass of this moving city
looking neither sly nor thieving
    merely tired
    vulnerable
pretty much how everyone looks
    riding the last Number 5 bus
going home after a long day of swiping
    all of us
    the tired—the vulnerable
    Oh man
home to where maybe somebody stands
    by the door
    neither sly nor thieving
    merely waiting

SWIMMING LESSON

You tell them it is easier to float in deep water
than in shallow water
though really you don't know why this is so
    —it's the same water
the same density that presses around you here
    as there
You instruct them to lower their face
    beneath the water
to catch your gaze under the cover of water
    never letting go
    never looking down
    to talk with your mouth closed
You tell them
it requires practice
to hover just so above the bottom
to kick in place
far over one's head
    suspended in such frail trust
buoyed by nothing but faith
    you tell them
it is how we must love this world

WANING GIBBOUS OVER
HIDDEN DRIVEWAY LAKE

The sonorous hush of a satellite dish
the rustle of chips from old blocks
the insomniac sputter of midnight bacon
the murmur and squeal of interest income
      dissipating—
it's *80s Nite* at the visitor center

It wasn't always so peaceful here
      across this designated wilderness area
there used to be a marker over near the hairpin
commemorating the exploits of those
who notched this arcadia into township
this acreage into lots
some have made this a destination in and of itself
but most just move on
the crumbs of their pretzels left under
the plaid cushions of our histories
      —our stories

The things we've kept sacred
      and the things we've pissed away—
      we don't dwell on
The old folks say that back in the woods
sits an old limestone fount—built by Vikings
      or Druids or Shakers
impotable now to those who thirst
all dead still and muck green—long emptied
      of its pennies

THE CUSTODIANS

We weary of these switchbacks
the glare of receptionists
the thinness of the air
at this altitude
rising in howls along stairwells
quivering the handrails
of the fifty-third floor
where we scour their bins of paper
smooth their berber of its frays
the maple laminate of its scoffs
mandalas of Tic Tacs and Post-its
mark the passage through these upper floors
where others like us have crossed before
our faces squinting in the high fluorescence
speaking in the languid dialect
    of atriums and fountains
We rest in the vacancy of cubicles
dream of release from the graying slosh
    and the static touch
from the harsh elevations of want

THE BAPTISMAL FONT

I've washed my hands of all of you
Goudy's skewer and Minion's slur
Christ—I've washed my hands of Minion
cleared my throat of Clarendon and Frutiger
rid this tongue of Palatino's serifed little lies
broken ranks from the rigid columns
     of Times Roman

I've touched the gash burned deep by Garamond
watched from its indents so many jump
     to their deaths
I've hyphenated the loss
and furrowed my brow with the italicization
swallowed hard every drop shadow
     of bitter almond

I've bathed in these crossed t's and dotted i's
doused the x seared across my face
scarred for life—I'm walking away
     from all of you
Don't ask me where I am going
     and don't write

SENIOR NIGHT GAME

Dayton Dragons 8—Peoria Chiefs 5
The old folks stop off afterwards for ice cream
at the United Dairy Farmers
carving away at the warm evening with frail
plastic spoons—dab at the thinning pool of days
with UDF napkins—nibble their sugar cones
in a circular motion downward
to its surprise chocolate end tip
—the best part

From behind the counter—all tight mint uniforms
and scoop clang—the UDF girls stare holes
into the clock face—roil the gunmetal water
poised to slam the lid on thirty-one awful flavors
itching to steal second base across the parking lot
where someone told them the Perseids
would be dropping rings tonight

Strategy counts for something—but in the end
it's all perseverance
those moments of softening rapture held close
in the squeeze play with a UDF vacuum cleaner
Maybe it's just not yet time for these girls
to grasp the sweetness that lingers in lingering
that blazes out softly in a circular motion downward
that saves itself for last
—the best part

PARTS & LABOR

Epitomizing the tenuous relationship
between man and machine—the Canon jammed
an 8 1/2 x 11 deep inside the manual feed tray
Morrie—the copier guy—arrived for servicing
kneeling down behind the Canon's open beige
slatted panel between us as I whispered

> *Forgive me—Morrie—it has been 15,221 copies*
> *since my last servicing*

Morrie shifted his weight and I smelled the wintergreen
and the disappointment in his slow exhalation
as I murmured

> *I have worked this machine in vain*
> *reducing what did not demand reduction*
> *and enlarging that which was just fine at actual size*

Morrie closed the front panel and inscribed my
penance across a thin yellow work order which he
had me initial

> ABSOLUTION

—the Canon's print button purred
its steadfast green glow—a dispensation of forgiveness
a facsimile of grace

Q & A with the Author

HIGH ENERGY AND MANY HATS:
AN INTERVIEW WITH GREGORY HISCHAK

GREGORY HISCHAK is an artist with a lot of energy and many interests, among them the visual arts, poetry, theater and music. He works actively in all of these mediums, bringing to life engaging, often funny, surfaces that shine past themselves into reflective interiors. In the 90s Hischak published a long running "zine" called *Farm Pulp*, and participated in the Seattle slam scene, becoming Seattle Grand Poetry Slam Champion in 1999. His theater pieces are being produced widely now on the East Coast. His play *Poor Shem*, included here in *Parts & Labor*, first appeared in the anthology *Best 10-Minute Plays of 2009* (Smith & Kraus). Pond Road Press took some time to question Hischak on topics of interest to working writers and artists, among them the conflict of earning a living while trying to produce art, the processes of creating a poem versus creating a play, the various intersections of his many artistic endeavors, and the path he followed from artistic pursuit to artistic pursuit, and back and forth among those arts, over the last thirty years.

PRP: *Parts & Labor* sparkles with insight about the intersection of making art and getting a living. You earn your living as a graphic artist. Could you comment on the balance, or lack of balance, between your artistic life and your work life?

GH: Well right there you've cut to the bone. So much of the work in this collection, and across all my work in general, is about the seeking of that balance. These disparate, rather jarring elements of my life are seeking some sort of harmony, or at least a place where they won't kill each other—and there's the origin of my writing.

I'm not particularly comfortable defining myself as a either a designer or a writer, if someone were to ask what I do. I'm sure a lot of artists live in this realm. The fact that I perform routine mundane tasks on a daily basis to allow me to exist in society, and the fact that

I am a poet—a commentator on society—means that I'm probably always going to be tightlipped about something. So maybe the writing reflects that: a tendency to use a distant sacred voice prodding the mundane or a clipped mundane voice prodding the sacred.

PRP: You use the word "sacred." Could you elaborate, even briefly, on what "sacred" means to you? What seems sacred to you and how do you know it when you see it?

GH: I'll define "the sacred" as that which rings true—and remains a universal truth across time, outside of time even. Examples would be a handful of Commandments, a tree, a landform, a masterpiece of any discipline from any culture. To speak from a sacred voice is to speak with a timelessness, say an ancient tribe of itinerant janitors who have hit the 53rd floor of an office building. To prod the sacred is to redraw *Starry Night* on an Etch A Sketch.

PRP: I've seen photos of your Etch A Sketch art, and am amazed at your fidelity to the masters you copy, like Vincent Van Gogh—on an Etch A Sketch. I'm not only delighted by such quirkiness and playfulness in your art, but I am also struck by the contrast it provides with the serious interiors of your poetry and plays. How did you come to "prod the sacred" using an Etch A Sketch? And what, for you, is the role of playfulness in art?

GH: Prodding the sacred with an Etch A Sketch is just the product of having had too much time on one's hands. The constraints of the instrument—the contour line, the gray on gray, the impermanent nature—they're all very appealing to me. That and the fact that you don't really draw with an Etch A Sketch so much as pilot it.

As far as playfulness in art, I think humans are by nature playful creatures even if prone to occasional cannibalism. To me art is the *playing with* of the human condition, throwing it against all those mediums to observe what it does—colored clay on a cave wall, a ballet, a painting, an ode. I think playfulness is just by nature present in art and sometimes it's expressed explicitly and sometimes it's obscured in very somber technique and palette—but it's still there.

PRP: Were you an incessant doodler as a child? How was it you were first drawn to the visual arts?

GH: I was drawn to visual arts at a very, very young age. At first it was the influence of siblings and the copious amounts of scrap paper my father brought home from work, later by the fact that drawing brought me attention in an otherwise pretty crowded household, and finally by the fact that my Aunt Mary gave me a quarter for every drawing I thrust at her. Doodling has always had a calming effect on me, getting me through very boring status meetings and poetry readings. The line is very powerful and I guess I'm kind of conscious of that in all my work—the expressiveness of the line that runs through. Doodling focused a lot of nervous energy into a tangible representation. I keep a lot of these drawings because I enjoy them and also I use them as a barometer to see if I'm going insane or not. Sometimes I can clearly see the iconography at play in them—concentric circles for boredom, cross woven textures connote restlessness, architectural structures hold suppressed anger, faces and totems mean I'm probably hungry.

PRP: Besides doing graphic arts and writing poetry and plays, you are also a guitarist, singer and songwriter. How does music fit into this constellation of activities in your life?

GH: Music is what shows up when the muse of poetry is absent and, honestly, it sticks around for long periods sometimes and can be a very powerful consuming tangent. It shares the social, community building aspects that working in theater brings and it is probably what I enjoy the most even though of all the hats I wear it's the one I'm least adept at—it's not my strongest voice. Also, problematically, at this point it's also a very one-way process with my songwriting never finding its way into stage work or poetry (while my stage work

Hischak's Etch A Sketch copy of Van Gogh's *Self-Portrait with Bandaged Ear and Pipe*.

Hischak's Etch A Sketch copy of Van Gogh's *Vincent's Bedroom in Arles*.

and poetry constantly cross-pollinate). However, songwriting is the most constraint-driven writing I do so I suppose it's exercising something somewhere inside.

PRP: How does music performance, the discipline of it, differ from poetry performance, as well as theater performance, and even the discipline of graphic arts?

GH: For me everything in music is just so much more critical in its presentation, even more critical than a script being performed on stage—though I say that as a playwright and not an actor. In playing music you have the responsibilities of melody, technique, presence, memorization—a lot of elements that you are personally responsible for and it creates a lot of pressure that makes it all gel or fall apart. Frequently it's just something in between.

I've never really thought of the relationship between my music and something as two dimensional as graphic design. In most ways they're apples and oranges but what I suspect ties them all together is just the sheer exercising of the creative process. The creation of a new work from the juxtaposing of existing elements is very exciting to me—joyful even—and perhaps I'm easily amused, but that seems to carry through all these disciplines.

PRP: Could you talk a bit about how you became interested in such a variety of arts and how your interests have migrated from emphasis on one art to emphasis on another, and then another, and how your interests move back and forth, as you hinted they do in speaking about your experience with music?

GH: I'd be tempted to dismiss myself as a dabbler but now I can see a logical progression to the last 30 years—stemming from my role as a graphic designer, and a graphic designer with free time on his hands. Using a photocopier and anything else handy as a medium, creating collage and assemblage work led me to book arts, art stamps and zines (low-run self-produced magazines). The zine work gained a following which led to some longevity and evolution: the writing content, at first just an extension of the graphic content, gradually became the dominant aspect of the publication. This then drew me into public readings at zine events and then into the poetry slam community which in turn was a springboard to writing specifically for the stage. All those elements that built upon each other remain in place. What changes is how I allot my time with these disciplines and sometimes my timing is prudent and sometimes I pursue dead ends. Also, I'm always drawn to these communities that arise over these mediums (the zine community, the slam community, a theatre company, etc.) and I've found comfort both in engaging them and in moving away from them.

PRP: You were involved in Seattle's slam scene some years ago. In fact, you were Seattle Grand Poetry Slam Champion in 1999. You, and your poems, always seem to perform well, many of the poems possessing both funny surfaces and serious interiors. How did the slam scene influence you as a poet and your ideas about poetry as art? Does poetry for you have to be both art and entertainment?

GH: When I started focusing on poetry I immediately embraced it as a performance medium. In spite of being a sort of tactile/paper person I saw the poetry on the page as just a necessary evil to get it to a performance state. Working in the slam community for those four or five years was, at first, very energizing and then very limiting. Slam performers tend to let their voices slip into a category— whichever category they win in—and it discourages evolution in their work. For me, slam was an effective editing tool and it always made me keep my eye on accessibility—I want my work to be accessible rather than to be just entertainment. In hindsight, that three minute time constraint that slam has now seems like a ridiculously long time for a poem go on.

Accessibility is the critical element between my readers and listeners and me. There is a natural block that many people throw up when they see a poem coming toward them and I like my work to approach them with a reassuring familiar voice. Once the idea has been ingested I'm fine to let it quietly explode.

PRP: Could you comment on how it's been to transition from being a poet who embraces poetry as performance to being a poet who produces both a performance as well as a written piece to be read in a magazine or a book?

GH: Both aspects of my poetry—the stage and page, as it were—still remain in place so it isn't so much a transition as a constant juggling. The work must be able to breathe both in and out of the water. What's evolved over the last few years is my desire to not let the poem have two faces. In the past I modified poems for one medium or the other and it made everyone involved a bit bipolar. The goal is now to have the identical piece work—line for line—aloud as well as on a page. Typographically, I'll try to reflect the cadence of the spoken piece; aloud I try to impart the feel of the piece on the page, the white space, the dangling word. Whether this all comes across or not I'm not the one to say, I only hope. Moving between both mediums is a wonderful development process as I tend to let a piece expand when considering its oral presentation and I tend to edit ruthlessly—well, never ruthlessly enough—when I have it back on the page. Still, that constant expansion and contraction allows a lot of elements into the poem and with a little luck the strongest elements remain.

PRP: What gets you going when you write a poem? How do you create the poetic thread of the poem when you compose?

GH: While not particularly a storyteller, at heart I'm a builder of stories. The story is important to me and I'm initially sucked into a new poem by the potential story it wants to say. In building a poem the early drafts are always concerned, usually too concerned, with the thread of that story. It's critical, in my process, to get that line down on paper and these early drafts are clunky and repetitive and can be totally encased in scaffolding for a long time. At some point I remove the scaffolding and address the language of the poem, word by word. The tone may shift, the stanzas get reassembled, everything is shuffled and reshuffled and then I take it out for a test drive and someone says "cut the first half" —and they're right. Apparently writing a poem is similar to how you should pack for a long trip— choose just the very minimal amount of items you think you'll need, put them in the suitcase, and then take half of them out.

PRP: At this point in time, what place does poetry and the writing of poetry occupy in your life? Who are some of the poets who have influenced your work?

GH: Well, we're frequently not on speaking terms but I'm nonetheless in a committed relationship with poetry. I co-curate a poetry reading series (in West Dennis, MA), I'm asked to participate in poetry events, I sporadically teach or perform work in high schools, where I live I'm perceived as a card-carrying poet and, really, I guess I am. There is always a folder of poetry drafts that I'm hauling around in case that free moment arises and poetry is the base from which all my other writing springs.

The poets who influence me, and I say that in the present tense because I remain receptive to influence, are poets I know, whose work I've heard or hear regularly. Peter Pereira and Kathleen Flenniken are two Seattle poets whose voices were very influential— not that I sound like them but they brought the importance of voice to the fore for me. I'm always challanged by the reading of poetry books because I approach them with an editing hat on that I can't take off. I think James Tate is the only poet whose work on the page I found unassailable and complete—and his work is sort of anti-poetry, so go figure.

PRP: I have had the good fortune to have seen several of your plays performed. *Poor Shem*, **a vivid depiction of both the closeness and the distance of work friends in their workaday milieu, seems quite modern in its timing and its exhibition of**

comic wit, not unlike Beckett or Stoppard. It's a piece that drills down into the unmistakable substance of our lives, in this case our work lives. What's it like to be a playwright and to work with a director, cast and crew to realize what must be both a personal and a shared vision of a work like *Poor Shem*?

GH: In the case of *Poor Shem* it's a very short and very buttoned down shared vision. Here it's largely a matter of fealty to the script and attention to the pacing of the text. *Poor Shem* doesn't really beg (currently) for major reinterpretation. That said, it's always different when I see it staged because there are a few handles on the piece that allow the actors and director to grab hold and to run with it. The chemistry of the three actors defines the piece almost as much as its rhythm and the director's decisions on how abstractly to treat the setting always make it a slightly different play from production to production. In my larger works like *The Center of Gravity* and *Volcanic in Origin* where I always stumble on structure, the director and dramaturg were indispensable partners in the play's development. Here it really becomes an assemblage of a lot of different expertise—all with a shared vision and you move away from being the poet and become part of a larger organism. It's an exhilarating experience that poetry can't touch—though everything was born of the poetry.

I've always found the leaping back and forth from poetry to theater to be a very natural fit with how I develop work—expanding and contracting a piece of writing. Enlarged, given movement and having a defined space around which words are played out—you've created theater. Reduce those words down to their sparse little nuggets of language—you've distilled it down to poetry.

ACKNOWLEDGEMENTS

Grateful acknowledgment is made to the editors of the following publications in which these poems first appeared, some in slightly different versions:

"The Assistant" appeared in *Bellingham Review*.
"The Culling" appeared in the *Atlanta Review*.
"Closure" appeared in *Pontoon: An Anthology of Washington State Poets*, Floating Bridge Press.
"Hidden Driveway Lake" appeared in *Green Mountains Review*.
"The Baptismal Font" appeared in the *Anthology of New England Writers*.
"The Temperature on Mercury" and "Firm" appeared in *Poems & Plays*.
"The Alluvial Hour" appeared in *The Mid-America Poetry Review*.
Poor Shem was staged by Northwest Playwrights Alliance, The Boston Theater Marathon, and Actors Theatre of Louisville. In print it appeared previously in the anthology *2009: Best 10-Minute Plays for 2 or More Actors*, Smith & Kraus.

Special thanks to all those who prop me up—from time to time or constantly—to my brother Thomas S. Hischak whom I've dedicated this collection to, and to Patric Pepper whose graceful stewardship and editing prevented me from driving this book into a ditch. Thank you to Ohio Arts Company and their kind permission to let images of their fine products appear in this collection. Thank you to Robin Clarke, my co-curator for the Poetry Session reading series for five plus years, to Kathleen Healy and Barry Sternlieb, for their voice and wit, to Lauren Wolk at the Cultural Center of Cape Cod who always has a poetry hat that fits me, and to Christine and Michael who know the value of a good kitchen table.

ABOUT THE AUTHOR

Gregory Hischak is a poet, playwright, musician and graphic artist. His writing has appeared in *Atlanta Review*, *Bellingham Review*, *Exquisite Corpse*, *Green Mountains Review*, *Mid-America Poetry Review*, *Third Coast*, *The Vincent Brothers Review* and *Zyzzyva* among others. His long-running zine *Farm Pulp* was widely reprinted, and several issues permanently reside in the Cooper-Hewitt National Design Museum and the New Museum of Contemporary Art in New York City. His plays have been staged by the Humana Festival of New American Plays, the Source Festival, Portland Stage Company, City Theatre, and Boston Playwrights' Theatre, among others. His play *Crows Over Wheatfield* was nominated for a 2008 Pushcart Prize, and his play *The Center of Gravity* was the 2010 Winner of the Clauder Prize for New England Playwrights. With Robin Clarke he co-curates the Poetry Session reading series in West Dennis, Massachusetts—just down the road from where he lives, works, teaches, and gets by.

COLOPHON

Had I been able to wrestle it from the sea
this would have been my ending poem

My defining poem—maybe even my title poem
set in an old style Garamond or modern Bodoni

The poem reeled in off the coast of Chile
or from the western edge of the Tasman Sea

Its white italics thrashing—its vowels lustrous
its consonants a bristle of harpoon barbs

Its weights of such aquiline grace that here—
at the bow of this bar stool—I can only dream of

Everything that might have been said
I watched breach and descend into the deep

Hidden until it chose to surface and feed
close to where I would be waiting

ABOUT POND ROAD PRESS

Pond Road Press was founded in 2003 by Mary Ann Larkin and Patric Pepper, and publishes poetry chapbooks that often include author interviews. Among our authors are Meredith Holmes, Jack Gilbert, Piotr Gwiazda and Gregory Hischak. Look us up on the Internet at www.pondroadpress.com.

ALSO FROM POND ROAD PRESS

Tough Heaven: Poems of Pittsburgh, by Jack Gilbert

From his North Beach days to this day, Jack Gilbert was and is, in his life and in his poems, uniquely fine. This collection is a good way to test my claim, and serves as a way into all his other volumes. I recommend him to my students and other friends and he never fails to captivate them. I mention his name to almost any poet and the shock of recognition wells up in their eyes, their mouths, their faces, and shimmers.

— David Madden, author of *Abducted by Circumstance*
and *London Bridge in Plague and Fire*

Messages: Poems and Interview, by Piotr Gwiazda

Piotr Gwiazda comments on the title of his poetry chapbook *Messages*. "The first association will be - perhaps inevitably - with the phone, email, and text messages we send and receive on a daily basis. Also the messages that 'pour out of various devices' (as in Muriel Rukeyser's poem): news stories, speeches, alerts, warning labels, traffic and weather reports, TV and radio commercials, those targeted ads on Google and Facebook. Communications overload - but with a touch of magic to it. Again, we are both consumers and producers of messages: we post, we blog, we update, we upload. But I was also thinking about the broader connotations of the word. After all, messages can be exchanged in the course of a simple conversation."

PRP books are available at Amazon.com,
BarnesandNoble.com, and from Pond Road Press.

www.ingramcontent.com/pod-product-compliance
Lightning Source LLC
Chambersburg PA
CBHW032133090426
42743CB00007B/584